MW00896615

Blockchain
The Complete Step By Step Guide To Understanding Blockchain Technology

MARK WATNEY

© Copyright 2017 by Mark Watney - All rights reserved.

The follow eBook is reproduced below with the goal of providing information that is as accurate and reliable as possible. Regardless, purchasing this eBook can be seen as consent to the fact that both the publisher and the author of this book are in no way experts on the topics discussed within and that any recommendations or suggestions that are made herein are for entertainment purposes only. Professionals should be consulted as needed prior to undertaking any of the action endorsed herein.

This declaration is deemed fair and valid by both the American Bar Association and the Committee of Publishers Association and is legally binding throughout the United States.

Furthermore, the transmission, duplication or reproduction of any of the following work including specific information will be considered an illegal act irrespective of if it is done electronically or in print. This extends to creating a secondary or tertiary copy of the work or a recorded copy and is only allowed with express written consent from the Publisher. All additional right reserved.

The information in the following pages is broadly considered to be a truthful and accurate account of facts and as such any inattention, use or misuse of the information in question by the reader will render any resulting actions solely under their purview. There are no scenarios in which the publisher or the original author of this work can be in any fashion deemed liable for any hardship or damages that may befall them after undertaking information described herein.

Additionally, the information in the following pages is intended only for informational purposes and should thus be thought of as universal. As befitting its nature, it is presented without assurance regarding its prolonged validity or interim quality. Trademarks that are mentioned are done without written consent and can in no way be considered an endorsement from the trademark holder

Table of Contents

Introduction

Congratulations on downloading this book and thank you for doing so. Technology is growing rapidly, and some may find that keeping up with new innovations is a full-time job; in fact, the time-consuming process of learning and implementing new technological advances, even if they will ultimately save time and money, is one of the prime reasons why individuals and companies choose not to use them. This book will help you understand one of the most exciting technological advances in the decade, an innovative new technology that is truly revolutionizing how business transactions from all sectors are made. That technology is blockchain.

The following chapters will discuss in great detail the history of blockchain, beginning with ideas that date back to the early 1990s that ultimately helped lead to its inception. It will then delve into the original use of blockchain — development of the virtual currency known as Bitcoin. It will look at other technologies that were spawned by blockchain, such as smart contracts, as well as other applications that utilize blockchain technology, such as Ethereum and Blockstack, and possible innovations in the commercial sector that would utilize blockchain. Next, it will look at functional limitations and challenges of blockchain, including legal and ethical issues that arise from the technology, before exploring how individuals can get started with blockchain and make money off of it. Some of the information will be very technical, while some will be about history or practical information on how to utilize the technology.

There are plenty of books on this subject on the market, thanks again for choosing this one! Every effort was made to ensure it is full of as much useful information as possible. Please enjoy!

Chapter 1: Background Information

The Internet has traditionally run on a platform known as the client-server model. The client-server model is one in which a network is created between a main computer server and numerous client computers that are connected to it. The main computer server potentially stores the data and information for a particular Internet application, such as a bank's online banking service, as well as a database of personal information. The bank's customers can log in to their online accounts by entering their usernames and passwords, which is information stored by the main server in a database. The computer on which the customer is accessing his or her bank account online becomes a client of the main server. The client computer and the main server can then interact in such a way that the client can access the program run by the server. In other words, the bank's customer can access his or her account online.

The client-server model has enabled many businesses to thrive by creating websites that users can use to access their own accounts. However, the systems created by this model have proven themselves, time and again, to be susceptible to hackers. In 2001 and 2002, a Scottish hacker named Gary McKinnon hacked into the United

States' Military computer system. The damage from the hack was so extensive that the military had to close down 2000 computers for a full 24 hours, and the cost of the damage was nearly three-quarters of a million dollars. From 2005 until 2007, Albert Gonzalez led a group of hackers to steal the credit card and other account information from 90 million TJX customers. While companies are opening their wallets to fund firewalls and other new layers of cyber security to protect their websites and their customers, hackers prove over and over again that they can overcome these defenses and access critical information.

Furthermore, the client-server model is prone to temporary and sometimes permanent failures due to problems with the main server. If the main server experiences a technical problem, such as overheating, or becomes infected with a virus or some other computer bug, the entire network may be unable to operate until the problem is resolved. If too many clients are trying to access the server simultaneously, the server may be unable to accommodate them; as a result, users may not be able to access sometimes-critical information in a timely manner. These failures, while not usually catastrophic, can impair a business's ability to function at its full potential.

Blockchain works differently. While the traditional client-server model allows client computers to connect to a centralized server that stores all of the program's information, including the personal information of customers, blockchain runs on a decentralized system of nodes. Nodes are individual computers — they can be spaced out all around the world — that host the blockchain program. Some of the largest organizations that utilize blockchain technology have close to 10,000 computer nodes. Some companies that utilize blockchain actually have plans to put nodes into space!

This vast system of computer nodes means several things. First, it means that there is a vastly smaller probability of network failure. A client-server network may utilize only one server computer, so if that one computer fails for whatever reason, the entire network can go out. If one computer node on a blockchain goes out, the effect may not even be felt because there are thousands more that are still operating. A complete failure of the node network would require a truly catastrophic event of global proportions.

Second, it means that there is virtually no possibility of the blockchain system being hacked. If a client-server network utilizes only one server, a hacker only has to break into that one computer in order to bring down the entire network or fraudulently access the personal information of millions of people. However, with thousands of computer nodes servicing the blockchain, the hacker would have to either access every single computer simultaneously without being detected, or collude with every single person that operates a node. Therefore, the system is all but impenetrable.

Third, it means that the information stored in the blockchain cannot be changed. With a client-server network, a hacker, or even a less-than-ethical employee, can change the information stored in a database. However, because the blockchain is hosted on so many computers, the information cannot be changed without the collusion of the entire network. Since this is extremely unlikely to happen, the information stored in the blockchain is virtually immutable.

While blockchain technology does have some challenges and limitations, which will be discussed later, possibly its most inherent, defining feature is its built-in security. Time and again, it has proven that its security features are far superior to those of the traditional client-server network; as such, it can redirect the funds that individuals and companies would normally spend on security measures into more profitable spending.

Chapter 2: History of Blockchain Technology

Although blockchain was initially developed to support the conception and development of Bitcoin, the virtual peer-to-peer currency, some computer scientists had ideas that helped lead up to the blockchain revolution. Understanding the history of how blockchain was developed over the two decades before the advent of Bitcoin, will help enable an understanding of the defining features of blockchain — especially the timestamp — and why they are important.

During the late 1980s and early 1990s, a technology that allowed users to modify pictures was being used more and more to alter and edit pictures used in the media. This trend raised serious ethical and legal questions about how to verify that digital information has not been tampered with. In January of 1991, computer programmers Stuart Haber and W. Scott Stornetta published an article in the *Journal of Cryptology* entitled "How To Time-Stamp A Digital Document." The article raised legitimate concerns about the transfer from businesses performing transactions via a paper-based media to a digital-based media. Businesses and other organizations would need to find a way to verify when the document was signed, changed, or modified in any way. They needed to ensure that their digital documents could not be tampered with.

The solution proposed by Haber and Stornetta was that rather than time stamping the media used, such as the document itself, businesses should timestamp the actual data involved in the transaction. They proposed a method that would prevent individuals, even with the collusion of a professional time-stamping service, from being able to retroactively pre-date or post-date a document. Their ideas would contribute to blockchain's ability as a digital ledger to store the timestamps of individual transactions in such a way that they cannot be altered.

During the 1990s and early 200s, Ross Anderson, an expert in computer security based at the University of Cambridge, published several papers on the need to increase security capabilities. He noted that financial institutions are particularly susceptible to failures in internet security and suggested that security breaches are not primarily the result of failures in cryptoanalysis but the result of failures in implementation of the security systems. In other words, a paradigm shift regarding Internet security was necessary. He also brought to light problems with established protocols in cyber security, showing how contemporary security cyber security systems are highly susceptible to hacking.

In 1998, Michael Doyle filed for patent number EP19980949485, an invention for computer security systems that would implement standard chain-of-evidence protocols to digital systems. Hearkening back to the paper published by Haber and Stornetta in 1991, the invention would allow for individual pieces of digital data to be time stamped without the need for third-party verification. The system would use pairs of public and private keys to ensure that the timestamp could not be tampered with.

Other theoretical designs would help lead up to the blockchain revolution. In 1998, Nick Szabo, an expert in contractual law in the digital world, laid out a framework for a digital currency known as bit gold. Users would have to solve complex cryptographic puzzles; the solutions would become part of the next puzzle, thereby creating a public peer-to-peer chain in which users would have to work together and agree upon each other's solutions. The timestamp system that he used eliminated the problem of double spending, in which one digital token is used twice. The plan for bit gold was that it would not be connected to a centralized registry for its value; like real gold, its value is not based on legitimation by a central authority. Bit gold was never implemented, but the peer-to-peer chain technology would be crucial for the development of blockchain. In the year 2000, the computer programmer Stefan Knost laid out designs for a technology that would use secure chains for cryptographic information. In doing so, he helped lay out the foundation for the implementation of blockchain technology.

On August 15, 2008, a request for patent US20100042841 A1 was filed by Neal Kin, Vladimir Oksman, and Charles Bry. The patent was for a secure encryption technology that would utilize two keys to encrypt messages through a chain of encryption. While the three men denied any connection to Satoshi Nakamoto, the pseudonym for the creator of Bitcoin, the technology for the patent closely resembled what came to be known as blockchain.

On October 31, 2008, Satoshi Nakamoto released a white paper outlining how his peer-to-peer virtual currency — Bitcoin — would function. It would run on a secure system that would utilize digital signatures as well as timestamps of transactions. The timestamp idea goes all the way back to the paper published by Haber and Stornetta in 1991, which proposed verifiable, tamper-free timestamps for individual pieces of data rather than for the entire document. The time-stamped transactions would be hashed together into a chain that could not be undone without changing every previous transaction.

Rather than have a centralized authority or be based on a central host computer, the chain would run on a system of nodes, individual computers that people voluntarily provide to host the chain. This would provide the CPU power necessary to power the chain and keep it running. It would also create a peer-to-peer network. The peer-to-peer network is essential to blockchain technology because it is a natural, built-in audit system as well as protection against hackers. It functions as an audit system because, as previously stated, the time-stamped transactions cannot be changed without changing every previous transaction. What this means is that in order for the timestamps to be tampered with, every single individual in the network would have to be in collusion. It functions as a protection against hackers because the lack of a centralized computer host prevents an individual from cracking the system. One hacker can break into a host computer and manipulate the data, but the entire network of individuals would have to collude with each other in order to break the decentralized blockchain and manipulate the data. To this day, while various Bitcoin wallets and exchanges have been hacked to the tune of millions and millions of dollars, the blockchain technology has prevented Bitcoin itself from being hacked.

Not long after the implementation of Bitcoin, blockchain technology was separated from the concept of the virtual currency as programmers began to realize the huge potential behind it. New programs other than

Bitcoin that utilize blockchain are called alternative chains, or altchains. As of 2017, 15% of all banks are utilizing blockchains to secure their financial transactions. Other altchains are showing promising ways of preventing voting fraud, better tracking patient health, and even building a new Internet!

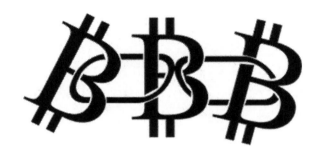

Chapter 3: Other Technologies Spawned from Blockchain

While the technology behind blockchain was developed and implemented by Satoshi Nakamoto for the express purpose of creating Bitcoin, its conceptualization hearkens back nearly two decades prior. Many programmers worked on the concept as a means of improving cyber security. Today, blockchain is the most secure piece of internet technology and has applications that extend far beyond Bitcoin. It is being used to develop a slew of new technologies that are not only simpler than those provided by the traditional client-server network, but that would be all but impossible using it.

Smart Contracts. One piece of technology that was spawned by blockchain is something called a smart contract. Smart contracts digitally facilitate the exchange of items of value — money, investments in a fund or the stock market, etc. — without the need for a middleman, such as an escrow service (however, one may be provided just in case there is an unforeseen dispute between parties). In fact, the public blockchain itself functions as the witness to the signing of the contract.

17

When two parties agree to draw up a contract between them, the information from that contract becomes encoded as a block in the blockchain, which is public and visible to all computer nodes on the network (see more about that under "The Mechanics Behind Blockchain"). However, the identity of the individual parties bound by the contract remains private and anonymous.

For example, imagine that John is selling company stock, which Jim wants to buy. John and Jim agree to complete the purchase of the stock using a smart contract. They both sign it and use a date exactly one month in the future as the date at which the stock will be transferred to Jim. John inputs into the smart contract the data that will automatically confer ownership of the stock, and Jim deposits into the smart contract the money that will be used to pay for the stock. When the agreed-upon date at which transfer of ownership will be conferred, the ownership of the stock will be automatically transferred to Jim, and the money that Jim deposited will be automatically paid to John.

As another example, imagine that Jim is a real estate broker selling a house that John wants to buy. Both of them agree to complete the transaction using a smart contract. John pays a deposit on the house directly into the smart contract; meanwhile, Jim puts the digital entry key into the smart contract. When the actual key arrives and John can get into his new house, Jim gets paid the funds that were held by the smart contract. While the process of buying a home is certainly more complicated than that, this example demonstrates how a smart contract functions.

Smart contracts are behind the Ethereum phenomenon. Ethereum is an open-source software that uses smart contracts to facilitate the building of decentralized applications. The creator of Ethereum, Vitalik Buterin, originally worked for Bitcoin and realized that the programmers behind it were not utilizing the technology to its full potential. He developed a platform that allowed users to develop their own apps without having to create an entirely new blockchain; instead, they plug into the Ethereum blockchain. An online currency known as the Ether is used to pay for transactions that utilize the Ethereum network. As an indicator of how successful the Ethereum network has been, the value of the Ether has grown exponentially.

Some people have suggested that smart contracts be used in voting; rather than having to stand in line at a polling station, individuals would be able to vote on their computers with almost zero possibility of fraud. They could also be used to ensure cash on delivery by delivery services such as UPS and Fed-Ex. The projected potential for smart contracts is virtually limitless; more and more businesses, as well as the federal government,

19

Mark Watney

are exploring the possibilities behind it.

Proof-of-Stake. Satoshi Nakamoto's original blockchain conception, as laid out in the white paper that went live on October 31, 2008, utilized a technology known as proof-of-work (see more under "The Mechanics Behind Blockchain"). This protocol was established to ensure that an actual transaction was performed and keep bots out of the network. Proof-of-work has proven to be very useful; however, at best it is not efficient, and at worst it is extravagantly wasteful because it uses an extraordinary amount of processing power. Newer blockchain technologies are beginning to operate on a slightly different protocol known as proof-of-stake.

While proof-of-work requires that computational work is performed in order to legitimize a transaction, proof-of-stake requires that the person proves ownership (or stake) of whatever is being exchanged. One method of proof-of-stake is for the individual to, as part of the transaction, send money already in his or her possession back to his or herself. Another method involves the use of digital signatures.

One advantage to proof-of-stake over proof-of-work is that proof-of-stake requires significantly less energy and processing power. Another advantage is that it is safer. The Ethereum network is converting its protocol from proof-of-work to proof-of-stake; it created a proof-of-stake system known as CASPER in order to better facilitate transactions in a more energy-efficient manner.

Blockchain scaling. Blockchain scaling is still largely in the conceptual stage, but it holds great potential for making blockchain technology more efficient and accessible. Currently, every single computer node on a blockchain network must validate a transaction; this process is inefficient because it uses a large amount of energy. Blockchain scaling would allow the network to determine how many computer nodes need to verify a transaction; the nodes utilized would then be limited to that number.

One challenge associated with blockchain scaling is figuring out how to ensure that the network remains as watertight and bulletproof as it currently is. The public ledger hosted in the blockchain functions as a built-in audit that helps prevent fraud; further, for a hacker to bring down the network, he or she would have to access every single computer node simultaneously or have the collusion of every single user. Considering that this is virtually impossible, the blockchain network is all but impenetrable. While limiting the number of computer nodes involved in transactions has the potential to scale back on the amount of energy used, it could also compromise blockchain's most basic security feature. Before blockchain scaling can be implemented, companies and organizations that wish to utilize it will have to deal with this security challenge.

Chapter 4: The Mechanics Behind Blockchain

This section provides detailed technical information on how a blockchain actually works. Even if the information is confusing, one can utilize services such as Ethereum or Lisk to help implement his or her own ideas into a blockchain.

Stuart Haber and W. Scott Stornetta were the first to conceive of the idea of blockchain technology in 1991 when they published a paper on the necessity of being able to verify timestamps on digital media. Their solution called for a network of users, referred to as clients, each bearing a unique identification number. The network of clients would function as a built-in audit; more than one individual would have to be involved were someone to try to falsify the timestamp data.

Using complex mathematical formulas, they developed an idea known as a hash function. The hash function would create a unique value for the data needing to be time stamped. The data would also have a unique digital signature that would tie it back to the creator. Haber and Stornetta claimed that their idea would eliminate the margin of human error and incompetence by outsourcing the entire timestamp function to a computer program.

Fast-forward 17 years. In 2008, blockchain was developed with the idea of being able to consistently verify the data implemented in a series. Because Satoshi Nakamoto originally created blockchain to process financial transactions for his digital currency, the need to verify the timestamps was of paramount importance. Otherwise, the technology would enable double-spending, a scheme in which a user makes two or more rapid transactions so quickly that both are processed from the same digital token; this allows the equivalent of using one dollar to purchase two one-dollar items because the program was not able to respond quickly enough to the first transaction to prevent the second transaction. Accurate and quick time stamping of the transactions prevents double spending from occurring. In this way, blockchain built on the conceptions introduced by Haber and Stornetta in 1991.

With this extensive collection of timestamps, blockchain functions as a digital ledger. A ledger is a collection of financial and account information, which is precisely what the original blockchain — Bitcoin — was created to keep track of. However, most ledgers can only be operated by one user at a time. If two users are working on the same ledger, say QuickBooks, separately, they cannot have the most up-to-date information because one user does not know what the other user has done or what information has been updated. In order for two individuals to work separately on the same ledger, one of two tedious, time-consuming processes must occur. The first option is that they must work on it one at a time, and each user routinely send the other user the updated ledger so that the second user can work on it with the updated information; the second user will then send it back to the first user and wait for the first user to finish working on it and send it back. The second option is that they work on it simultaneously, then go through the painstaking process of reconciling the two different sets of information that they both implemented. Both of these options are not only tedious and time-consuming but also leave large margins for human error.

Blockchain works differently. It allows multiple users to work on it simultaneously while continually updating the data that each user sees so that every user is working with real-time information. In this way, it is like a Google spreadsheet. Microsoft Excel is a great tool for managing large amounts of information, as long as there is only one person at a time who needs access to that information. A Google spreadsheet updates the information entered into it in real-time so that multiple users can access and manipulate the information simultaneously.

Before getting into the technicalities of how blockchain

technology works, there are some terms that need to be defined.

Blocks. A "block" in a blockchain is like a cell in a spreadsheet that holds a piece of data. The data usually contains a timestamp for when the transaction occurred; as Haber and Stornetta pointed out in 1991, the ability to verify the timestamp on a business transaction is of utmost importance for companies and businesses to prevent fraud. Every transaction is compiled into its own block with the timestamp data. Each block is connected to another block, which contains the data for the transaction made immediately before (for the block that was created previously) and for the transaction made immediately after (for the block that was created after). All of the blocks that are linked together form a chain, hence the term "blockchain."

Nodes. A node is a computer that is connected to the blockchain and is able to view all of the information in it. Multiple nodes are spread out across a vast number of different users, all of whom have access to the data in the blockchain. Every time a new transaction occurs, the data is sent to every computer in the node network; the nodes automatically assume that the longest chain is the most up-to-date and correct.

Proof-of-Work. Proof-of-work is a way of verifying that a transaction was created meaningfully rather than by a robot. In a blockchain, a proof-of-work is usually a verifiable piece of information produced by an algorithm. Every block in a blockchain has its own proof-of-work that must be verified by a node. When the node verifies the proof-of-work, the block becomes public as part of the blockchain.

Key. In blockchain, a key is like a translator that translates complex algorithms and cybertext into language that is readable and meaningful to the general public. Keys are used to encrypting the data in a blockchain and then to decrypt it; this provides a high level of security to the users that utilize the blockchain. The security of the blockchain system is directly connected not only to the size of the network of nodes but also to the strength of the keys.

A public key is used to send data to other users on the blockchain. A private key is like a digital signature for a user on the blockchain. If someone's private key was accessed by another user, that user would be able to deplete the other person's entire Bitcoin account by sending all of the Bitcoins to himself or herself. Therefore, while public keys are exactly what the name implies — public — private keys should be kept secret.

Input. In a blockchain, an input is basically a value for every single incoming transaction that a user has ever received within that blockchain. These values are all stored as blocks in the blockchain. In terms of Bitcoin, an individual's input is the amount of Bitcoins that he or she has ever received.

Output. In a blockchain, an output is basically a value for the outgoing transaction that a user wants to make. The output is directly tied to the input in that a user cannot send something that he or she does not have. For example, say that a user has an input of two Bitcoins and wants to send somebody half a Bitcoin. The half-Bitcoin would be the output value, and it would be taken from the input value of the two Bitcoins.

Hash Function. A hash function is essentially a computer program that creates a summary of the larger amounts of information that needs to be stored; this enables the system to store copious amounts of data without overwhelming its memory. A cryptographic hash function, which is what is utilized in the blockchain, is a unique type of hash function that that converts an input message into a string of alphanumeric values. The value produced is known as the hash value or the digital fingerprint. The probability of two separate input messages creating the same hash value is extremely unlikely.

How a Blockchain Transaction Works

Understanding the terminology above will help enable an understanding of how a blockchain transaction works. A transaction is a piece of data that is signed with an individual user's digital signature; that data becomes embedded within a block in the blockchain.

When a user on the sending end tries to make a transaction, a new block that contains the data for that transaction is created. The block is connected to a previous transaction in which that user received a transaction; for example, if a user is attempting to make a transaction that will send an amount using Bitcoin, the blockchain will reference the previous output value in which that user received an amount of Bitcoins. The blocks will stay linked to each other in the blockchain. The attempted transaction is then signed with the sending user's private key; this functions as a digital signature to verify that this user was, in fact, the person authorizing this transaction.

The block is time stamped, which proves that the data in the block was present at the time that the transaction was authorized by the user. This is a further protection against fraud. The timestamp is publically broadcast as a hash value.

The input value that was created by the sending user's attempt to make the transaction is then converted to an output value. This output is used to derive the user's public key from the private key; the public key then uses an algorithm to transform itself via a hash function into a unique value, thereby creating the sending user's public address that is visible on the blockchain's nodes.

The use of the public addresses was Satoshi Nakamoto's solution to needing a central authority or other third parties, such as a coin mint, to verify the transactions. The public broadcast means that all participants on the blockchain system must agree to the transaction, thereby providing a built-in audit to protect against fraud.

The block that was created when the sending user began the attempted transaction is then sent to the network of nodes for verification. The verification is based on a set of protocols, also known as proof-of-work, which can change over time. The protocols in the proof-of-work verification can include ensuring that the block is less than 1MB in size; that it has a value of greater than 0 but less than 21 million; that a real value is present for both the input and output of the transaction; that the output value has not already been used by the sending user; and/or that there is a matching transaction. If the protocols are not entirely met, the transaction may be denied.

Once verified, the node that received the information for the transaction will then relay the block to all of the nodes in the network, thereby becoming a block in the blockchain. The data contained in the block cannot be changed because the timestamp protects against retroactively trying to undo the transaction. Further, the block becomes linked to subsequent blocks that were created at a later time; therefore, for any hacker to change the data in the block, he or she would have to change every other block leading up to it. The ownership of whatever is being transacted — Bitcoins, electricity, personal identity records — is then transferred to the person receiving the transaction.

All in all, the time required to process a blockchain transaction can take anywhere from a few seconds to ten minutes or longer. The lengthy transaction time is connected to the high degree of security that is inherent in the blockchain system; a user is exchanging an ultra-fast transaction for a highly secure transaction.

How Mining Transactions Work. Some blockchain applications, especially those that run on virtual currencies, require that the currency is mined, or generated before it can be added into the pool of currency in circulation. Computers that are used to mine the currency take blocks of transactions and transform them into mathematical puzzles. The miners compete with each other to find a solution to the puzzle. The first miner to solve the problem by creating the correct hash value gets a reward, usually a predetermined amount of the virtual currency being mined.

The mining process is actually what enables the blocks created by users engaging in transactions, such as sending and receiving Bitcoins, to be verified. The miners use the information contained in the blocks to create the hash value, which is used to validate the information and prevent it from being altered. If any information in the blocks is changed, the value of the hash will also change; therefore, the hash value is critical in maintaining the network's security.

Solving the hash is what generates the Bitcoins, so miners try to solve as many hashes as quickly as they can. Because computers are very good at the algorithms used to create the hashes, blockchains use a proof-of-work to keep the currencies from being mined too quickly.

Chapter 5: Blockchain Applications

The decentralized, impenetrable structure of blockchains is so innovative that some have dubbed it a new type of Internet and claim that it is spawning a similar revolution. The decentralization aspects fit the core values — such as empowering individuals rather than multinational corporations and big banks — of many enthusiasts associated with the blockchain community, especially that of Bitcoin. Innovators with the aforementioned mindset are using blockchains to create applications and organizations that help facilitate and implement those values. At the same time, it is being used by large banks and organizations who likewise want to benefit from all of the features of blockchain. It even has potential uses in government, such as preventing voter fraud and reversing low voter turnout.

Bitcoin. While the ideas and development of blockchain technology stretch back nearly two decades before Satoshi Nakamoto published his white paper, the concept was originally implemented to facilitate the creation of Bitcoin. Bitcoin is a virtual, peer-to-peer currency that is not regulated by any government. It does not exist in hard form, such as cash; rather than being minted by a treasury or other centralized regulating body, it is mined by programmers who solve complex mathematical and computational problems to release blocks of Bitcoins into the Bitcoin pool.

Because there is no centralized financial body regulating Bitcoin, its value is not set or predetermined by any one authority. Rather, it derives its value entirely from consumer demand for it. When more users buy and make transactions in Bitcoin, its value goes up. And consumer demand has been high: In less than a decade, its value has gone from less than a penny to thousands of dollars.

Governments have made many efforts to regulate the virtual currency. In 2016, the United States Internal Revenue Service declared that Bitcoin was property and subject to taxation as such. Some European governments, such as the United Kingdom and Switzerland, have helped facilitate the use of Bitcoin by the mainstream public; while these efforts have made Bitcoin more accessible, some worry that governments are meddling in the virtual currency and attempting to regulate it. However, one defining a feature of Bitcoin, as with blockchain technology in general, is that it is decentralized and unregulated (see more under "Limitations of Blockchain").

Ironically, Bitcoin helped prove its viability as a legitimate currency through scams and illicit trading. Silk Road was a website created by Ross Ulbricht in

2011. It used Bitcoin's anonymity (at the time, a Bitcoin user did not need to disclose his or her true identity to engage in Bitcoin transactions) to facilitate trading in illegal drugs. After the website had been shut down in November 2013 and Ulbricht arrested and sentenced, the FBI seized millions of dollars in Bitcoin assets. With the American government now in possession of Bitcoins, albeit through a criminal scheme, its legitimacy could not be denied.

Another scandal that ironically helped solidify the standing of Bitcoin was BitInstant, an online startup led by Charlie Shrem and Gareth Nelson. Under the company, Shrem engaged in money laundering but denied that this was a criminal offense because Bitcoin is not a true currency. The FBI disagreed, and Shrem pled guilty to money laundering.

Despite these scandals, academics and researchers have found that ever since November 2013, Bitcoin has been used mostly for mainstream purchases of legitimate commercial goods rather than in the "sin marketplace," which included activities such as Silk Road purchases and gambling. It has even been used to pay university tuition and buy houses. Bitcoin's popularity continues to grow, both among the world's elite and the general public.

The blockchain technology allowed the currency to be completely decentralized and be virtually impenetrable to potential hackers. In this way, Blockchain was the perfect platform for implementing a revolutionary idea such as Bitcoin. One may think that blockchain and Bitcoin were made for each other. In fact, they were. However, the uses, capabilities, and applications of blockchain go far beyond Bitcoin.

Ethereum. Besides Bitcoin, the most well-known and profitable blockchain application that has been created was Ethereum. Vitalik Buterin, who founded Ethereum when he was only 22 years old, previously worked for Bitcoin and as such was familiar with the capabilities and potential of the blockchain technology. He felt that it was not being used to its full potential, and when his coworkers didn't support his innovative ideas, he went on to develop his ideas by creating Ethereum.

Ethereum is a platform that app developers can use to create their apps on blockchain technology, but with the ease of not having to create their own blockchains. Creating a new blockchain from scratch is an extremely complex, intensive process that can be inefficient for purposes such as designing individual apps. Ethereum allows developers to create their apps with all of the benefits of blockchain — such as the public ledger and other high-security features — in a way that is efficient and feasible.

Ethereum functions through the use of smart contracts via something known as the Ethereum Virtual Machine

(EVM), which essentially functions as its own computer programming language. Like Bitcoin, Ethereum runs on a virtual currency; this one is known as the Ether. The Ether is used to fund transactions and developments on the Ethereum blockchain. The Ether is like Bitcoin in that it is a decentralized virtual currency. However, unlike Bitcoin, it is tied to an actual commodity: the blockchain that allows developers to create new apps.

Counterparty. Counterparty is a computer platform for the decentralization of finance. Most finance is tied up in centralized, heavily regulated institutions such as Wall Street banks and the New York Stock Exchange. The financial catastrophe of 2008 made many people aware of the dangers of having so many assets and securities tied up on Wall Street; in the time since little regulation to prevent another crash has been implemented. However, with innovations such as Bitcoin enabling financial activity that is not regulated or dominated by big banks, Counterparty is attempting to facilitate a revolution in enabling peer-to-peer financial exchange that doesn't need middlemen. Instead of waiting for policies and regulation that would weaken the power of major financial institutions, Counterparty seeks to enable individuals at a grassroots level to build free markets.

One feature of Counterparty is that users can create their own digital currency; this currency functions within the Bitcoin blockchain. Users can then enable their new currency to be exchanged in a peer-to-peer manner on the market; they can also issue dividends for individuals who invest in their currency. The value of the new currencies is set against the Bitcoin, and the currency can be exchanged for its Bitcoin value. Like Bitcoin and Ethereum, Counterparty has its own currency: the XCP. Unlike Ethereum, it runs on the Bitcoin blockchain.

Besides allowing users to create their own currencies, Counterparty allows users to create and execute smart contracts as part of the Bitcoin blockchain. Rather than Bitcoin, the smart contracts are implemented using the XCP. XCP is also the currency used to determine voting rights and other internal issues within Counterparty.

Lisk. Like Ethereum, Lisk is a platform that enables the development of web-based applications on a blockchain. While Ethereum uses its own programming language — the Ethereum Virtual Machine — Lisk uses JavaScript. JavaScript is more widely known by programmers, so they can more easily use Lisk to develop their apps; they do this by creating side chains off the main blockchain. This enables users to effectively create their own blockchains while still operating on the Lisk network. They can use Lisk to develop their own online stores, execute smart contracts, perform financial transactions, deliver messages — basically, anything that a blockchain can do.

Lisk also has its own virtual currency, the LSK. Rather than using proof-of-work like Bitcoin (see "The Mechanics Behind Blockchain), which is the time-consuming part of the blockchain exchange process) or even proof-of-stake like Ethereum (see "Other Technologies Spawned by Blockchain"), Lisk uses a modified proof-of-stake to verify its transactions; this enables LSK transactions to be completed in a matter of seconds. Like the Ether on the Ethereum network, the LSK is used to fund transactions on the blockchain.

Like other blockchains, Lisk is open source, which means that its code is made freely available to the public. This enables its complete decentralization, another important feature of a blockchain. These two features work together to ensure that a third-party mediary or middleman is not necessary to perform a transaction on the network. Like many other blockchains, Lisk runs on virtual currency rather than government-backed national currencies.

Augur. Augur is a software that was built on the Ethereum network. It seeks to utilize collective intelligence to make predictions of future events. Collective intelligence refers to the combined wisdom of a group of people that collaborates together rather than the intelligence and ability of an individual, even an expert.

Augur users buy into the market of a future event prediction, such as who will win a sports game or a government election, by purchasing shares that are equal to the probability of that event occurring. For example, if there is a 60% chance of a particular candidate winning an election, the cost of the share to buy into that prediction is 60 cents. The amount paid and the prediction is stored as a smart contract inside the blockchain. When the event actually occurs, the smart contract expires, and users who accurately predicted the future event are compensated.

The result of the public buying into cheap shares of the prediction market is that the collective intelligence generated enables better forecasting of future events. The decentralized nature of the blockchain technology on which Augur works means that the data cannot be manipulated by any central or governing authority, but rather is entirely crowd-sourced. This crowdsourcing plays into the values of the creator(s) of Bitcoin, the original blockchain, by relying on a peer-to-peer network rather than a centralized authority to regulate the market.

Blockstack. Blockstack is an open-source software that is built into the Bitcoin blockchain. It essentially built a new, vastly more superior Internet that runs on blockchain technology. Programmers can build apps onto the Blockstack chain, which then becomes a part of the Blockstack network. The result is an Internet that is as decentralized, secure, and incorruptible as Bitcoin.

While the Internet as most people today know it is prone to massive data hacks and security breaches, Blockstack apps utilize the security of blockchain technology to protect all of the personal information of a user. Rather than being run by a large central organization, the apps are run locally off of the user's device. This locality feature means that personal information is not stored in a main central database that can be hacked, thereby leaking compromising the identity features of countless people. Instead, a local private key is used to store private information.

Because Blockstack is open source, any individual or corporation can create a namespace or domain, as no centralized governing authority exists to prevent someone from doing so. In fact, the open-source feature prevents governments from censoring websites; in order to do so, they would have to effectively shut down the entire Bitcoin network — a virtually impossible task, because they would have to either have the collusion of every single operator or be able to access every single node simultaneously.

In order to increase security and prevent spam from infiltrating the network, Blockstack is in the process of implementing its own digital currency. Even though it runs on the Bitcoin blockchain, it will not use Bitcoins as its token. It has also created its own browser, as well as an add-on that enables Blockstack capabilities in traditional browsers such as Google Chrome and Safari.

Traditional Finance. Although the blockchain technology was originally conceived of as part of a concept that would help decentralize the financial market, it is now being used to increase security in banks and other traditional financial institutions. While many banks are wary of the new technology because it hasn't been around long enough for its usefulness to be thoroughly tested, predictions estimate that by the end of 2017, 15% of all banks in the world will be utilizing blockchain. By 2021, that number is expected to grow to nearly 70%. Bank of America, Santander, and HSBC are already testing out ways that blockchain technology can be used and implemented to better serve their clients and facilitate financial transactions.

There are three primary ways in which banks and other financial institutions can make use of blockchain: retail payments, consumer lending, and reference data. Retail payments refer to the day-to-day transactions that individuals make using their bank accounts. This could be sending money to a friend online or making an everyday purchase for basic consumer goods. While those processes typically take days and sometimes even weeks to clear, blockchain could cut that process down to minutes while providing a high level of security.

Consumer lending, such as a bank financing a mortgage, credit card, or any other type of loan, could benefit from the smart contract innovation in the blockchain. The digitization of what is normally large amounts of paperwork and disuse of a mediary would decrease the time needed to process the loans as well as save the banks (and potentially the consumer as well) money. Reference data is the sharing of real-time information across businesses and institutions; the use of blockchain, especially smart contracts, could significantly eliminate the margin of error as well as the time involved to execute these tasks.

Challenges to implementing blockchain technology in the traditional finance sector include questions of how to prevent financial crimes such as money laundering and supporting terrorism. These challenges are real and crucial, especially considering that in Bitcoin's early days, its anonymity was exploited to finance the sale of illegal drugs through the Silk Road website and to commit several cases of money laundering. However, security measures, such as smart contracts, can be implemented to prevent this anonymous feature from being used to commit financial crimes.

Healthcare Technology. Two potential uses of blockchain technology within the field of healthcare technology are managing patient EMRs and facilitating insurance claims. An EMR, or an Electronic Medical

Record, is an electronic-based charting system that took the place of paper-based charts. The electronic-based records have the advantage of allowing patients and practitioners to track prognosis over time without having to shift through pages of paper files. Blockchains could be used to simplify the process of updating and maintaining EMRs. They could enable better tracking of data as well as cross-analysis. A blockchain's timestamp function prohibits the ability to retroactively change the time at which a transaction was performed, so insurance companies will be able to know exactly when a patient's diagnosis was made; this would prevent the companies from having to pay for pre-existing conditions. However, this potential would benefit the insurance companies more than the patients.

Health insurance companies could particularly use the smart contract aspect of blockchain technology to better facilitate their claims processes. The completely automated process would ensure that there is no question about how much the insurance company should pay out on a claim. The elimination of haggling over how much the insurance company should pay would reduce administrative costs, potentially saving money to both the company and customers.

Elections. Blockchain could potentially enable voting to occur online from a voter's own computer, rather than requiring that people line up at a polling station and fill out forms. Votes would be recorded as individual transactions and implemented into the blockchain, thereby preventing illegitimate votes. There would be no question of how many votes each candidate was given, as the users of the network would have access to the tally. This capability would eliminate the margin of error in elections and lengthy court battles that sometimes ensue, as in the case of Al Gore in Florida in 2000. The use of blockchain in elections could both reduce the possibility of voter fraud as well as help solve the problem of low voter turnout.

Chapter 6: Limitations and Challenges of Blockchain

While one might be led to believe that blockchain is a cure-all panacea for many of the woes that plague modern society, such as data breaches, government censorship, and providing an alternative to traditional government-backed currency, it does have limitations and challenges.

Energy Consumption. One of the touted benefits of Bitcoin and other blockchain applications is that they empower individuals in the mass public rather than large companies, which fuel modern crises such as global warming. However, the sheer size of a blockchain network means that its applications require large amounts of energy in order to function. In fact, one Bitcoin transaction uses *three thousand* times as much energy to process as a traditional financial transaction. With over 300,000 Bitcoin transactions occurring every day — and that number is growing — the total energy required to run the Bitcoin network is astronomical. In fact, by 2020, Bitcoin could use more energy than the entire country of Denmark. Its energy cost is so high that some researchers have suggested that eventually, the cost of generating new Bitcoins could actually lower the currency's value.

The Ethereum network utilizes a feature called Gas to keep track of how much energy is required for a transaction to be processed; the executor of that transaction then pays for the Gas in Ethers. The value of Gas to Ethers varies dynamically, and the network must constantly work to keep the two in balance. The programmers behind Ethereum implemented this system to ensure that the energy costs associated with the network are paid for pro rata by the users who generate those costs. While this business strategy has helped protect Ethereum and build up the value of the Ether, it has not solved the very real problem of energy consumption that contributes to global warming.

One possible solution is for these blockchain megacompanies to incentivize the use of alternative energy sources, such as wind and solar, to provide the energy necessary to power the systems. Not only would alternative energy significantly decrease energy costs and blockchain's carbon footprint, but it would also further facilitate the trend away from centralization: Alternative energy markets tend to be more local and decentralized than traditional fossil fuel companies.

Solarcoin is an innovative blockchain-based virtual currency that uses 0.0001% as much energy as Bitcoin. Its mission is to help incentivize the growth of solar energy. This currency is given away for free to people who produce solar energy as a way of offsetting the cost of implementing it as well as of helping to create new jobs in the alternative energy sector. Solarcoins can be exchanged in digital transactions much like Bitcoin, but without the carbon footprint.

Lack of Regulation and Standards. While one of the defining features of the original blockchain, Bitcoin, is that it is not regulated by a government or any central authority, and blockchain itself operates as a peer-to-peer network rather than on a central host computer, its growing use does leave some serious ethical questions about regulation and standards.

Firstly, there is the legal question of jurisdiction. Jurisdiction refers to what laws are in effect in a specific location. Programs that run on one centralized computer host can have challenges with jurisdiction, especially if a program operated in one jurisdiction is used illegally in another jurisdiction. The decentralized digital ledger system that blockchain uses means that every single computer node on which the blockchain operates could be in a different jurisdiction. Currently, there is no way to determine jurisdiction should a case arise regarding the legality of a particular blockchain.

Secondly, there is the legal question of what the blockchain's characteristics of "immutability" means, should a case arise in court. While cryptographic experts and blockchain enthusiasts tend to champion the fact that a blockchain is set up to avoid being tampered with, its immutability has not been legally defined. No court has officially recognized that a blockchain is impossible to tamper with.

Thirdly, there is the challenge regarding the European "right to be forgotten." The right to be forgotten means that any information about an individual that is stored in a database can be deleted, should that individual desire. However, blockchain's immutability means that that information cannot be deleted, which interferes with this right. The immutable feature of blockchain is so strong that rather than deleting personal information stored in the blockchain, the European policy may have to be re-worded to take into consideration the blockchain technology. If this were to happen, the above challenge of defining blockchain's immutability in court would have to be settled.

Fourthly is the question of how information stored in a blockchain can be held up in court. This is a potential challenge because blockchains are considered to be trustless — this means that no trusted third party or intermediary, such as a bank or other central authority, is required to verify the information stored in them. Courts would need to establish protocols for dealing with things such as smart contracts, or for declaring that assets held in a blockchain — such as Bitcoin or any other virtual currency — are indeed the property of the individual to whom the blockchain ascribes ownership.

Fifthly is the question of anonymity in blockchains. The Silk Road case is a prime example of how the anonymous feature of blockchains — in which a user may not have to reveal his or her true identity — can have a darker side. The Silk Road website was able to operate for several years, selling illegal drugs, before the FBI was able to arrest Ross Ulbricht, the man behind it. While Silk Road did not operate on a blockchain, Bitcoin, the currency of choice for the website, did, so users were able to purchase vast quantities of illegal drugs without any legal ramifications.

Integration with Old Technology. When new technology comes around, previously adapted technology must be either integrated into the new technology or replaced. For example, the DVD player made the VHS virtually obsolete. While the DVD technology was superior to the VHS and allowed more capabilities, such as immediately forwarding to the next scene without having to stop the tape and fast-forward it manually, its widespread adoption meant that people with large VHS collection had to convert to DVDs. While some VHS tapes could simply be replaced, some contained irreplaceable videos such as home movies.

As a new technology that is beginning to overtake previous computer platforms, blockchain needs to be able to integrate pre-existing programs, data, and legacy infrastructure before it can be used to its full potential.

Just as the DVD's replacement of the VHS produced challenges of integrating the new technology, so blockchain's overtaking of previous technologies and legacy systems is producing challenges of integrating the old systems into the new technology.

One potential solution is to manually upgrade legacy systems into the blockchain that the company wishes to use. Though costly and time-consuming, this process would adequately integrate pre-existing technology into blockchain. However, there is a potential for a significant margin of error. Another potential solution would be to build into blockchain a program that would enable automatic integration of previous technologies.

Chapter 7: How to Profit from Blockchain

All companies exist to make money. Even nonprofits and schools have to make money in order to survive. While blockchain technology was developed with the idea of giving power back to the common people — by enabling them to engage in peer-to-peer finances rather than having to use centralized banks — it has to be profitable in order to continue to exist and provide sustainable business models. Fortunately, there are many ways that blockchain is being used to generate income, and as blockchain's potential continues to be unleashed, more ways to generate income with it will be discovered.

How Blockchains Make Money

As discussed as a challenge for blockchains, the technology is incredibly inefficient and therefore can be expensive to run. However, blockchains have been extremely profitable for the individuals behind them. Estimates say that Satoshi Nakamoto, the mysterious identity behind the creation of Bitcoin, is in possession of one million Bitcoins. Now that Bitcoins are valued at thousands of dollars each were Satoshi to cash out by exchanging his Bitcoins for fiat currency, the value of Bitcoins could drop considerably for months, if not years. Vitalik Buterin, the creator of Ethereum, holds approximately 25% of all Ether, which amounts to 700,000 of the cryptocoins.

Other than creating a new currency and holding a large portion of it, which generates immense wealth as the value of the currency goes up, there are several ways that blockchains make money. One way is by charging fees for services. Many Bitcoin wallets and exchanges add a fee — sometimes 10% or higher — for using their services to purchase and store Bitcoins. Microsoft Azure has built a blockchain service that users can utilize for a fee.

Blockchain is also creating new jobs within already-existing companies, such as IBM. IBM has actually established a new department, Blockchain Business Development, which looks for new and innovative ways to implement blockchain technology. Its blockchain service is generating revenue by helping other companies integrate blockchain technology. Some industries and companies, such as the United States healthcare industry, are offering rewards for people who can come up with ideas and plans for how blockchain can be used to better track and analyze data and provide better services.

How to Profit from a Blockchain

There are many ways that individuals can profit from a

blockchain. One way is to build a blockchain and charge a fee for users to use it to build their own programs; this is how the entrepreneurs behind companies such as Lisk and Ethereum got started. However, that is a gargantuan task that may not be feasible without millions of dollars in capital.

With the value of virtual currency increasing so much, one of the most obvious ways to profit from a blockchain is to obtain tokens of virtual currency and wait for the value to increase. Consider the Norwegian man who, in 2009, bought $27 worth of Bitcoins. He forgot about them for four years; when he remembered them, their value had increased to nearly $900,000. Virtual currencies, especially Bitcoin, have entered the mainstream, and analysts and researchers now don't anticipate that they will disappear anytime soon. In fact, estimates predict that the value of Bitcoin may grow to upwards of $200,000 within the next five years.

There are a couple of different ways to obtain virtual currency. One is to pay the current exchange value for the virtual currency (effectively exchanging dollars or another fiat currency for virtual currency). This can be done by going to an exchange website, such as Kraken, BitQuick, or Coinbase, or to a Bitcoin ATM. Some of these websites allow users to purchase Bitcoins using cash, while others only accept debit or credit cards. LocalBitCoins enables users to meet in person at a mutually agreed-upon location to exchange Bitcoins. The virtual currency will need to be stored in a special online wallet, which functions essentially the same as a bank account. It tracks income and expenditures in a personal ledger and keeps an updated view of how much currency is in the account.

Another way to obtain virtual currency is to mine it. Virtual currencies don't have a central mint or treasure that produces them, so mining is the process by which new tokens of a particular virtual currency are generated. In reference to Bitcoin, special software is utilized to solve complex math problems. When the problem is solved, a block of Bitcoins is unlocked and added to the Bitcoin pool. Instead of paying for the currency, miners are usually rewarded with a percentage of the currency that they unlocked. Like every other process in the blockchain, the transactions completed by the process of mining must be verified using a proof-of-work or proof-of-stake protocol to ensure their authenticity. The process of mining helps to keep the network secure by verifying the transactions before they are added to the public ledger.

Chapter 8: Building a Mining Rig

A computer that mines for Bitcoins or other virtual currencies is called a mining rig. Mining rigs can be very profitable, especially if the currency being mined offers a reward to miners. However, a mining rig can also be very energy intensive, which for some can be cost-prohibitive. The most efficient mining rigs are connected to a source of alternative, renewable energy, such as wind or solar.

The mining rig can be used full time in the procurement of virtual currency or could be a computer dedicated to other purposes that only serves as a mining rig part time. Building a mining rig from scratch will require some special equipment be put together; the process is not unlike building a computer. While building the computer yourself will enable you to custom-design it for the mining operations that you want to do, as an alternative, you can purchase a computer; however, finding a computer with the exact specs for the mining operation that you want to do may be difficult.

The required materials for building a mining rig include:

Motherboard. A motherboard is the brains behind the computer; everything in the computer is connected to it, and it becomes the foundation of the mining rig.

Power Supply Unit. A PSU helps regulate the voltage inside a computer. It is regulated by the motherboard and, amongst other things, helps the computer start and reboot safely.

GPU Card(s). A GPU card is an electronic circuit that enables a computer to create images for display.

Case. The case is simply what all of the interconnected parts of the computer go into.

Random Access Memory. RAM allows a computer to recall information that it is storing.

Hard Drive. A hard drive is needed to store the software used for mining. It needs to have enough storage for the mining software.

Once you assemble all of the components of the mining rig (which is essentially building a new computer), you will need to decide which operating system your computer should run on. Possible operating systems include Windows, Linux, and Ubuntu. Look carefully at what your goals are for mining before you settle on an operating system. One operating system may be better for mining LSK while another one is better for mining Bitcoins. One operating system may be better for solo mining, while another one is better for pool mining. While all operating systems have their own unique benefits and drawbacks, you need to make sure that you use the operating system that will best help you accomplish your goals.

Next, you need to download the software that will be used for mining. For example, if you want to mine Ether for Ethereum, you need to download the EthOS app.

Now that you have your rig, there are a couple of different ways that you can mine. One is that you can go solo, which means that you are in a race against everyone else to get the correct hash, which will unlock the block of currency. Solo mining requires a lot of computing power and memory; one has to download the entire blockchain (imagine having to download all of the information behind Ethereum or Bitcoin onto your own computer). The alternative is pool mining, in which you collaborate with other miners to get the correct hash and unlock the block of currency. The rewards of the mining will be shared between you and the other users in your mining pool, but you will be able to get a steady stream of virtual currency without having to download the entire blockchain. You will have to determine which method is the best fit for you and accomplishing your goals.

Conclusion

Blockchain is changing many aspects of the modern world, such as how the Internet works, the definition of currency, and how businesses create their websites and apps. Blockstack, an application that operates on the Bitcoin blockchain, has used blockchain technology to design an entirely new Internet that is infinitely more secure. Users no longer need to worry about hackers breaking into a system and stealing their personal information. The advent of virtual cryptocurrency began a revolution in financial markets by challenging the notion that money is something that governments issue and regulates. Virtual currencies use blockchain technology to ensure that they are decentralized and regulated by a peer-to-peer network rather than by a central bank or treasury. Businesses such as banks are using blockchain in their websites to take advantage of the inherently high security features. Other businesses, such as Lisk and Ethereum, are using blockchains to enable developers to build apps. The potential that blockchain has to revolutionize even more aspects of the modern world is limitless.

Blockchain is still a relatively new technology that, while incredibly promising, still has a few challenges that need to be sorted out before it can be readily embraced by mainstream culture. It is replacing the client-server model, which is prone to hacking and failures, by operating on a vast system of computer nodes. However, its legal status needs to be defined so that, amongst other things, evidence procured from blockchains can be held up in court and people's rights, especially the European right to be forgotten, can be maintained. Further, it needs to be able to prevent financial crimes such as money laundering, as well as reduce its energy consumption and carbon footprint.

Despite these challenges, blockchain can be used to help people generate revenue. Some individuals have become significantly wealthy due to the explosive growth of virtual currencies, while some companies are profiting by enabling others to use blockchain. It can potentially be used in even more ways to help generate income.

Inevitably, blockchain will one day be replaced by an even more elegant, sophisticated technology with more capabilities that can help solve bigger problems. Until that day comes, blockchain provides many of the solutions to challenges facing the modern world.

Description

Computer technology is constantly changing; new technologies are created that solve a problem with pre-existing technology. A few years (or less) later, another new technology comes around that builds on what came before it while solving new problems. The technological revolution has empowered businesses to stay competitive and fueled the information age. However, keeping up with these trends can be both expensive and time-consuming. It seems that as soon as one new technology is mastered, another new one comes around to replace it. Many choose to not adopt new technologies because of the effort required in implementing them; as a result, they are unable to remain competitive.

This book will help you better understand blockchain, a new computer technology that is changing everything from how financial transactions are made to financial systems themselves. Unlike many other new technologies that emerge on the market, blockchain does not build on pre-existing technology. It actually created an entirely new model for how computer programs can run: in a decentralized, peer-to-peer, open-source manner that is not only virtually impenetrable but also does not require trusted mediaries to authorize transactions.

Blockchain's origins go back to the early 1990s, the time when the Internet was beginning to become more accessible to the public. The full concept was laid out in 2008 with Satoshi Nakamoto's white paper on his proposed cryptocurrency, Bitcoin. He developed the blockchain concept into a fully operational program that provides the best security features in all of cyber security. Some programmers saw that blockchain could be used for programs other than Bitcoin. They went on to develop powerful networks such as Ethereum and Blockstack, while other programmers began to experiment with other practical applications that blockchain had.

The potential of blockchain is enormous. It enables highly secure transactions that cannot be tampered with. One feature of blockchain, the smart contract, even ensures that all parties involved in a contract carry out their prescribed duties — without the need for any trusted third party or middleman! Thus, there is no need for haggling, disputing claims, or going back and forth on each party's responsibility. Adoption of this technology by insurance, financial, and other institutions carries the potential to save on administrative costs. Blockchain smart contracts could even be used in elections by enabling voters to cast their votes from home and automatically tally them in such a way that the final numbers are indisputable; this has the potential to eliminate voter fraud, reverse low-voter turnout, and the margin of error in counting votes. Even so, the potential that blockchain technology has is only beginning to be recognized.

In this book, you will find accurate, detailed information that will help you understand what blockchain is, how it is currently being used, and how you can use it. Topics covered include:

- The history of blockchain technology
- Other technologies spawned from blockchain
- The mechanics behind how blockchain works
- Applications for blockchain
- Limitations and challenges of blockchain
- How to profit from blockchain
- How to build a mining rig

The information presented is both useful and easy to understand. It will answer many of your questions about blockchain, and hopefully, inspire some creativity and imagination about how it can be used to help you meet your goals and needs.

46459632R00038

Made in the USA
Middletown, DE
31 July 2017